Treas
Not T

by Kim Tanaka
Illustrated by Lane Gregory

Editorial Offices: Glenview, Illinois • Parsippany, New Jersey • New York, New York
Sales Offices: Needham, Massachusetts • Duluth, Georgia • Glenview, Illinois
Coppell, Texas • Sacramento, California • Mesa, Arizona

Jake and Pam walked into Grandma's new apartment.
They saw boxes everywhere.
Grandma asked them to help her.

Grandma opened a big box.
"These are my treasures," she said.
"Please put these special things on the shelves. Be careful."
Jake and Pam started to work.

"This looks funny," Jake said.
"Why do you keep it, Grandma?"
"It is special to me," Grandma said.
"Your mother made it. She was just a little girl then. I think it is pretty."

Jake and Pam looked at the little man.
"Grandma likes this," Jack said.
"Mom made it," Pam added.
"Why don't we make something for Grandma?" she asked.

Jake and Pam went home.
They wanted to make something special.
"What can we use?" asked Jake.
"Whatever we find," Pam answered.

Jake and Pam found many things to use.
They found foil and cardboard.
They found clay and sticks.
They found buttons in bright colors.
They made something for Grandma.

They gave the artwork to Grandma.
It looked like a little house.
Grandma put the artwork on the shelf.
"Every day I will see it," she said.
"It is a great work of art!"